SOCCER SUPERSTARS

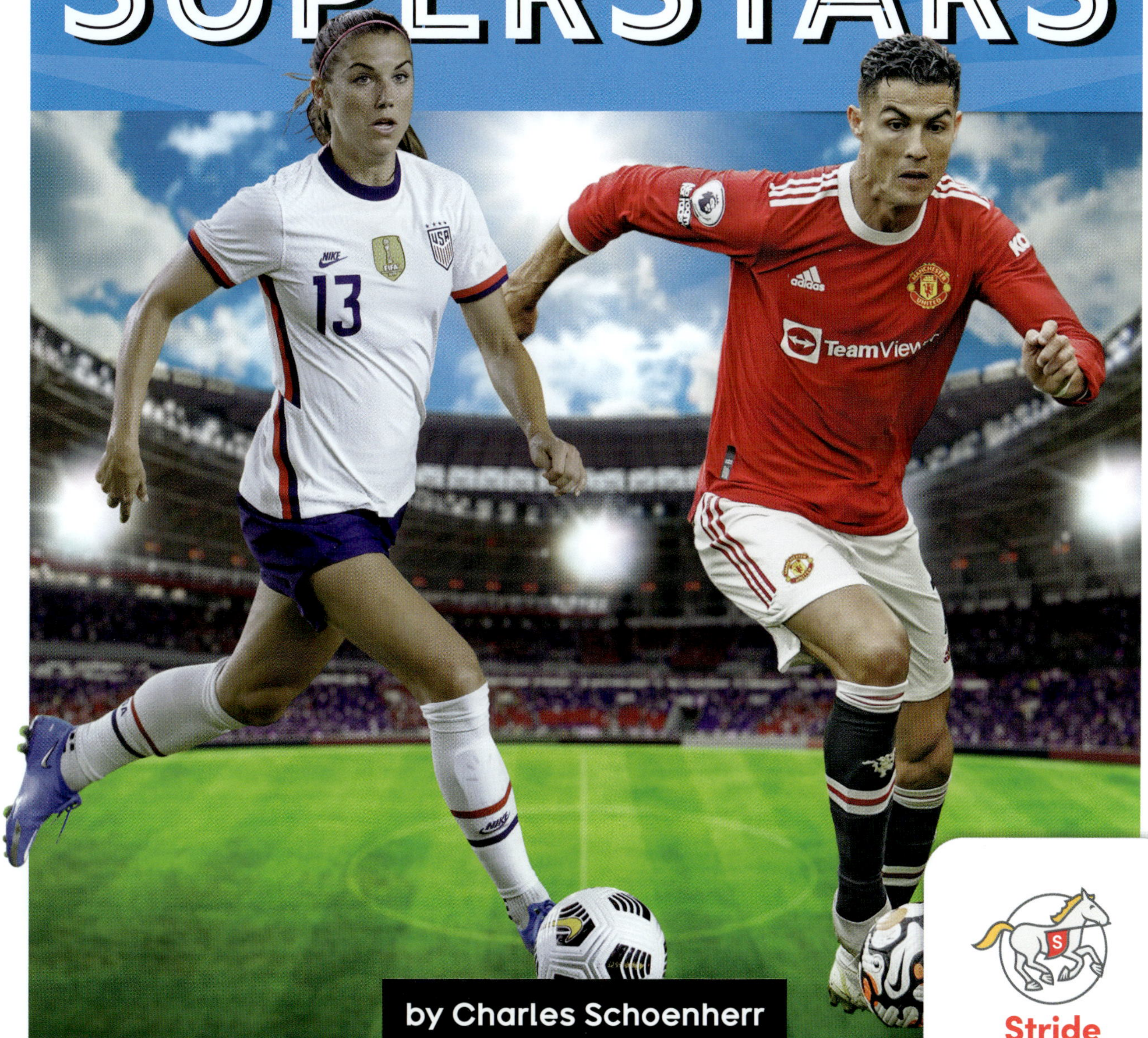

by Charles Schoenherr

Stride
An Imprint of The Child's World®
childsworld.com

The Child's World
childsworld.com

Published by The Child's World®
800-599-READ • www.childsworld.com

Photography Credits
Cover, 1: Dave Thompson/AP Images (left); Robin Alam/Icon Sportswire/AP Images (right); Zubar Malik/Shutterstock (bkgd). Interior: Dreamstime.com: Agenzia LiveMedia 4; Andre Ricardo 5; Natursports 7; Celso Pupo Rodrigues 8; Zeytun Images 15, 24; Lmediatore 17; Cosmin Iftode 18, 19; Steff22 20. Newscom: Jonathan Moscrop/Cal Sport Media 9; JustPictures/Sipa USA 11; Mutsu Kawamori/AFLO 13; Andrew Yates/Zuma Press 16; Daniela Porcelli/SPP/Sipa USA 25. Shutterstock: A. Paes 6; Gevorg Ghazarayan 10; Maxisport 12; Natrot 14; Ververidis Vasilis 21; AGIF 22; Oleksandr Osipov 23; Romain Biard 27; Cosmin Iftode 28; Ph.Fab 29.

ISBN Information
9781503858206 (Reinforced Library Binding)
9781503860797 (Portable Document Format)
9781503862159 (Online Multi-user eBook)
9781503863514 (Electronic Publication)

LCCN 2021952383

Printed in the United States of America

BRINGING THE WORLD TO YOUNG READERS 1968

SOCCER SUPERSTARS

TABLE OF CONTENTS

CHAPTER 1

THE TOP TWO

Soccer is the most popular sport in the world. Billions of people cheer for their favorite teams and players. When fans aren't watching, they might play soccer, too!

The world's best soccer players play on two teams throughout the year. They are paid to join a **professional** team, or "club," such as Barcelona FC. Top players are also invited to be on their own national team, representing their home country.

In the past few years, two of these players have stood out as true soccer superstars.

More than 30 countries have women's pro soccer, including Italy, shown here.

THE WORLD CUP

The best national teams play in the World Cup. The tournaments feature the national teams from every continent (except Antarctica), and are played every four years by both men and women. The picture shows the team from France after winning the men's World Cup in 2018. The United States women have won the women's World Cup four times and hope to be champs again.

Lionel Messi has scored more than 80 goals for Argentina.

Lionel Messi is from Argentina. He is widely considered to be one of the best players in the world. Yes, his name is pronounced as *Messy*! But he's certainly not messy on the field. Messi played 17 seasons with Barcelona, where he scored a league-record 474 goals. In 2021, he joined a different club team—Paris St. Germain in the French league.

Messi joined the Barcelona youth team when he was just 13. By the time he was 17, he was starring for the top Barcelona team. Messi helped them win 10 Spanish league championships. The team also won four **Champions League** titles.

Messi is a seven-time winner of the Ballon d'Or. That means "Golden Ball," and it's a trophy awarded each year to the top player in the world. Messi first won in 2009 and most recently in 2019.

No one has won more Golden Ball trophies than Messi.

Messi uses speed and dribbling skills to find room to attack.

What makes Messi so good? He uses his small size and **agility** to out-dribble and out-play his opponents. Messi has a magic touch with the ball at his feet. With the smallest of motions, he can zip past a **defender**. He also has a powerful left-footed shot. Messi can whip a hard shot past a goalie in a blink! But he also has a soft touch and will sometimes **chip** the ball over a goalie's head.

Teammates love playing with Messi. He is a fantastic passer, and puts his teammates in positions to score. He is a strong leader for his teams, too. Messi might be little, but on the soccer field, he plays like a giant.

Though he is left-footed, Messi can also shoot and score with his right.

The other player who can be considered a soccer superstar is Cristiano Ronaldo. He is from Portugal, and plays for their national team.

Ronaldo holds the record for most goals by any player—111 in international games like the World Cup. He also led his country to the European Championship in 2014. Ronaldo cried for joy as he raised the trophy for his nation.

A familiar sight: Ronaldo celebrating after scoring for Portugal.

Ronaldo's dribbling skills make him hard to defend.

Ronaldo began his career at home in Portugal. He moved to England to play for the Manchester United team in 2003. That's where he became an international superstar, twice winning the Premier League player of the year award. In 2009, Ronaldo joined Real Madrid in Spain. He led them to three Champions League titles. This great player holds the record for most Champions League goals!

After four seasons with Juventus in Italy, Ronaldo rejoined Manchester United in 2021. His fans there were thrilled to have him back. He scored two goals in his first game!

What makes Ronaldo so good? A big reason is his fitness. He works out all the time. He always eats the right food and won't drink soda. He once removed a soda bottle from a table as he began an interview so that he would not be photographed with it. He also won't get a tattoo, because that would mean he could not **donate** blood.

Ronaldo is taller than most players, and he jumps well. This lets him score many goals with his head. Ronaldo also has great speed to outrun defenders. And his **stepover dribbling** moves have confused many opponents. Look for his highlight videos to see soccer brilliance.

Ronaldo shows off his fit form after a goal.

Which way will he go? Ronaldo played for Manchester United in the 2021 Champions League.

CHAPTER 2

A WORLD OF SUPERSTARS

Soccer is played with eleven players on each side. Teams use different **formations** to try to win games. All the players are skilled at kicking, **trapping**, and controlling the ball. They can hit it with their heads, too. When an opponent controls the ball, all eleven players become defenders in one way or another. When a team has the ball, everyone tries to help score a goal.

One way to line up is with four defenders, four midfielders, and two forwards, sometimes called strikers. A goalie plays at the back.

Whatever formation a team uses, fans will see similar position names. Let's take a look at the best strikers, midfielders, defenders, and goalies around the world.

Strikers

Brazil's great star Neymar might be the next superstar. He plays for Paris St. Germain in France. Neymar is second only to Pelé in goals scored for Brazil. And Pelé is often considered to be the greatest player of all time! Neymar is known for his incredible style and his accurate right-footed shot.

Neymar has scored more than 70 goals for Brazil's national team.

Sam Kerr (left) and her Chelsea teammates celebrate another goal.

Australian Sam Kerr plays for Chelsea in the Women's Premier League. Experts think she just might be the top female player in the world. Kerr has also scored more goals in the National Women's Soccer League (NWSL) than any other player. Very few defenders can slow down her race for the goal.

One of the youngest players on this list of soccer superstars, Kylian Mbappé (em-bah-PAY), is a French powerhouse. He plays on Paris St. Germain with Messi and Neymar. In 2018, he helped France win the World Cup. Mbappé is an amazing dribbler with great speed.

Another young star is Vivienne Miedema. Before she turned 25, she had set an all-time record for goals scored for the Netherlands. She also had set the career scoring record for the Women's Super League in England!

In 2018, Mbappé became only the second teenager to score in a World Cup game.

Tall and strong, Lewandowski can score from any angle.

Robert Lewandowski is a Polish striker who also plays for Bayern Munich in Germany. A tall player, Lewandowski is known for his ability to score using his head from **crosses**. Lewandowski has such a cool style of play, he is the choice to take many **penalty kicks**. He helped Bayern win 10 league titles and two Champions Leagues. In 2020, he was named the world player of the year.

England is where professional soccer began, and its national team has a super striker. Harry Kane does one thing really well—score goals. He always seems to be in the right place at the right time. For his national team, Kane is among the all-time leading scorers. For his club team, Tottenham, he has led the Premier League in goals four times. Showing that he can share, too, Kane led the league in assists in 2020-21!

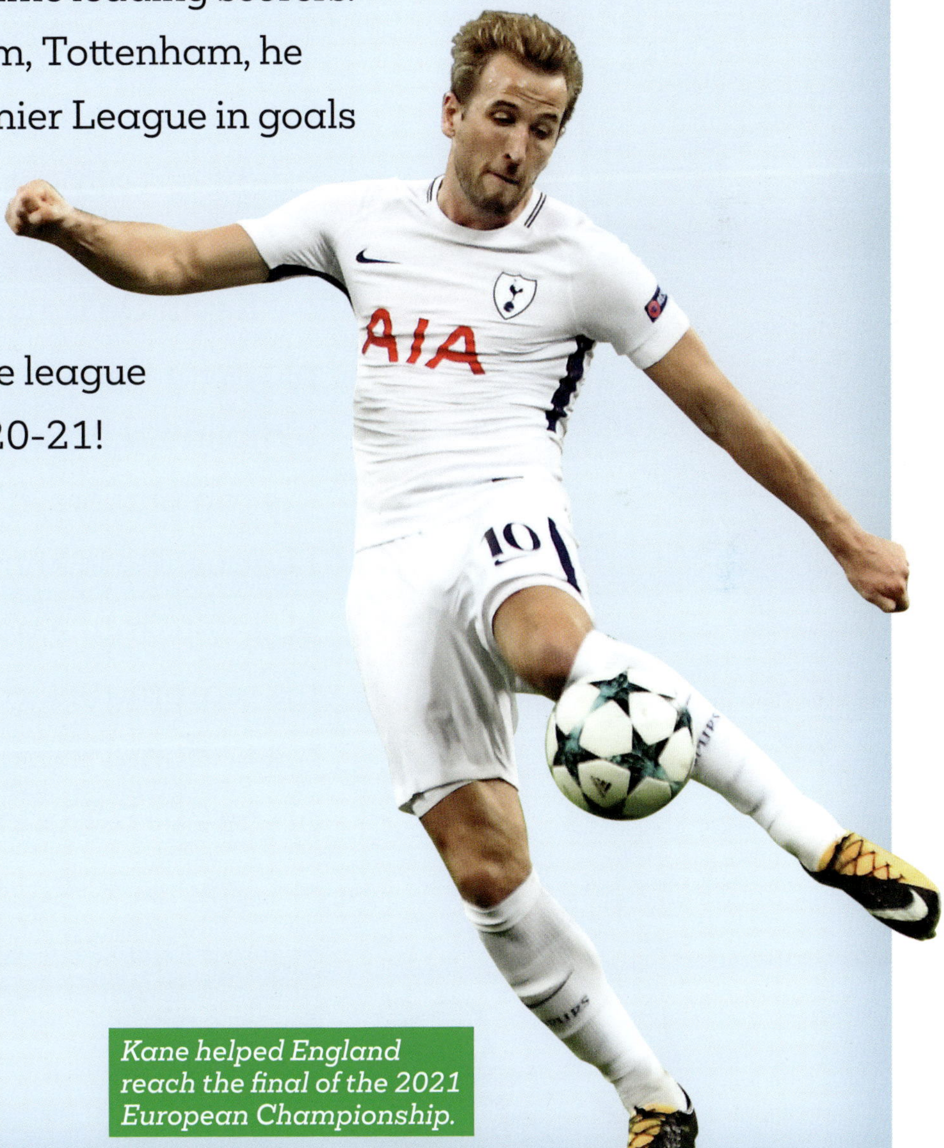

Kane helped England reach the final of the 2021 European Championship.

Midfielders

Midfielders play between strikers and defenders. They control the direction of the game by passing the ball to other players. Midfielders have incredible **endurance**. They might run almost 10 miles in one game!

Kevin De Bruyne of Belgium plays for the Manchester City team in England. He is among the top players in the Premier League. He is known for his ability to make perfect passes to his teammates. He also helped his national team reach the final of the 2018 World Cup.

De Bruyne is like his team's quarterback, directing the action.

Germany's Dzsenifer Marozsan has won just about every kind of soccer trophy. In 2016, she led her nation to its first Olympic gold medal. With the French club Lyon, she won the Champions League. Her all-around skills put her on the World Team of the Decade for the 2010s.

Marozsan scores more goals than most midfielders.

Defenders

Defenders are the last line of defense before the goalie. They work hard to prevent strikers and midfielders from scoring. Without a good defense, a team can't expect to win many games!

Thiago Silva is the **captain** of Brazil's national team, and a member of the English club Chelsea. Silva plays center back, directing his fellow defenders. Silva has great skill with the ball, but his real talent is for stopping attacks before they can get started.

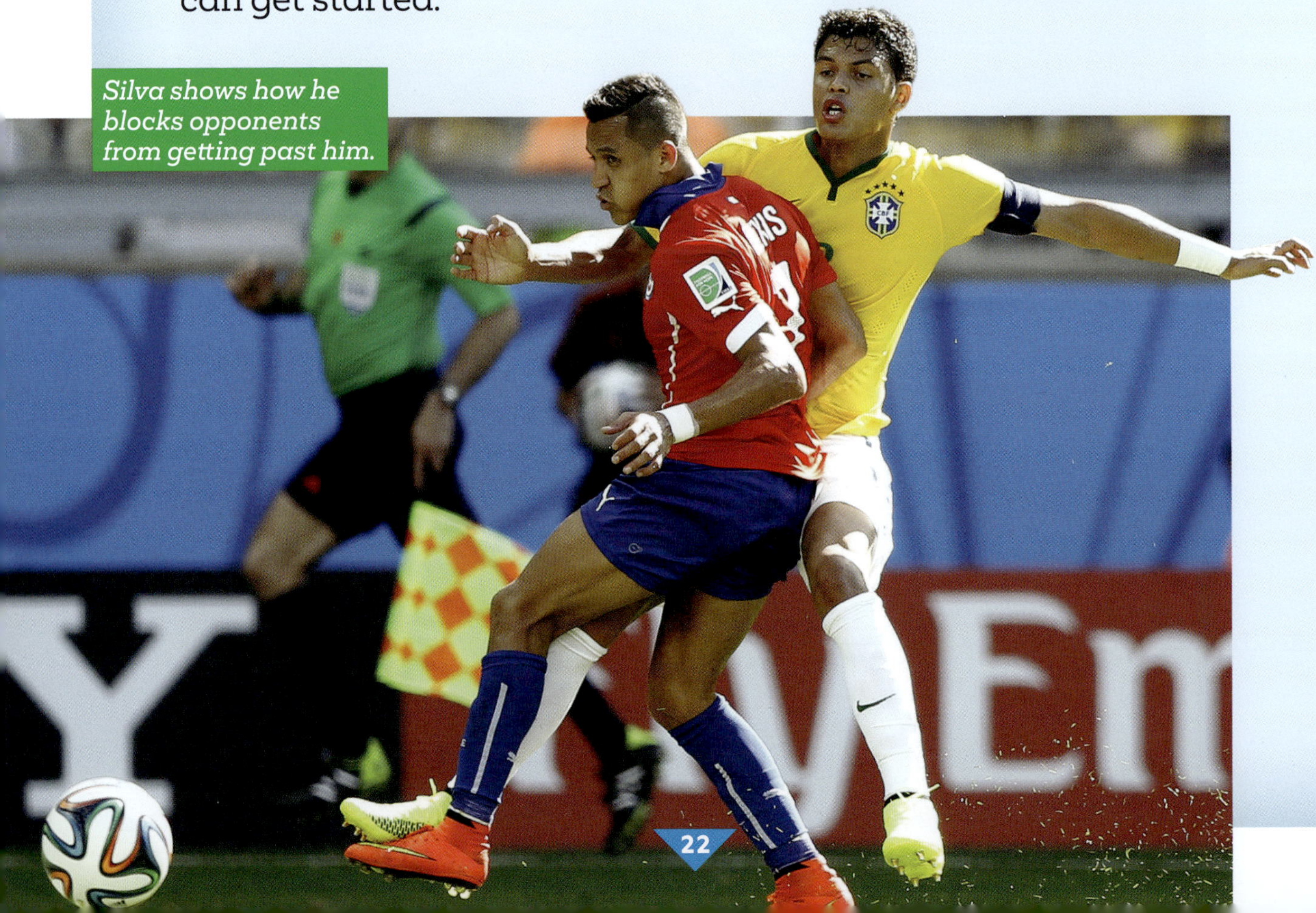

Silva shows how he blocks opponents from getting past him.

Rúben Dias is also a center back. This defensive star from Portugal plays for Manchester City in England. Dias is known for his strength in the air and his field vision. After he takes the ball from an opponent, he is great at finding teammates racing up the field for a pass.

Wendie Renard is the top woman defender in the world. At six feet, two inches (1.87 m), she uses her height to **dominate** the **penalty box**. Her great work has helped her club Lyon win seven Champions League titles.

Renard is used to lifting trophies for her French club.

Goalies

Goalkeepers, or goalies, are the last line of defense. They are the only players who can use their hands to block goals. A great goalie is like a wall—nothing gets past them. Some of the best goalies are also the tallest players on the field, giving them extra reach to stop the ball.

One of the best is Alisson, who, like most players from uses just one name. Liverpool's fans love calling it out after one of his amazing **saves**. He is known for his calm, cool attitude. He is also good with his feet, so he can help teammates with big passes down the field.

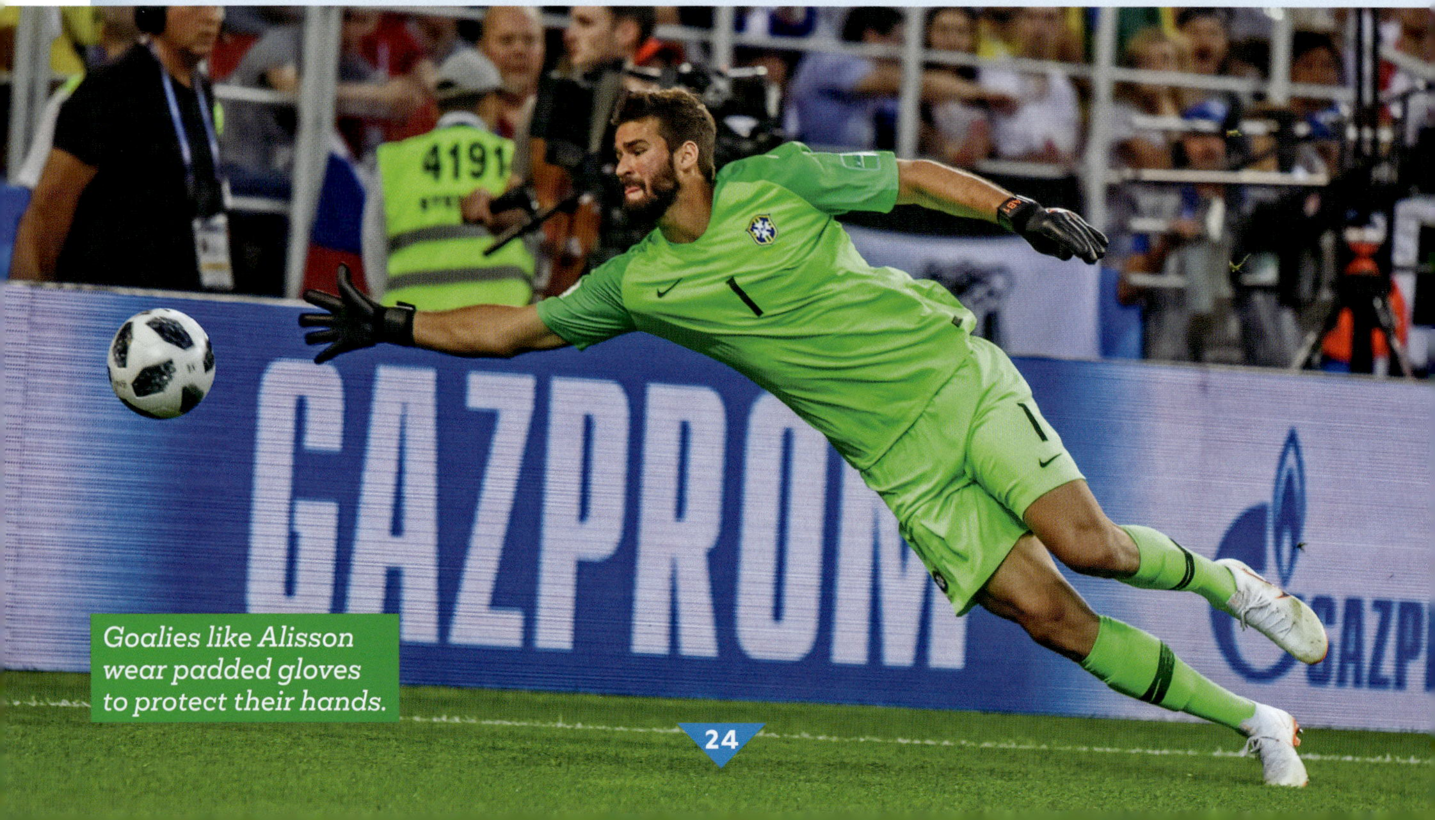

Goalies like Alisson wear padded gloves to protect their hands.

Endler shows off her quickness as she dives on the ball.

Jan Oblek is another top goalkeeper. He is the captain for the team from the country of Slovenia. His club team is Spain's Atletico Madrid. Oblek's skill at reaching for the ball in the air breaks up many goal-scoring chances.

Height and skill make Chile's Christiane Endler the top woman goalie. She started out playing basketball and only started soccer later. Endler was a fast learner and now stars for Paris-St. Germain and her national team.

CHAPTER 3

AMERICAN HEROES

America has some incredible soccer players, too. The U.S. Women's National Team is the best in the world. They have won four World Cup titles and four Olympic gold medals. They have star players at every position on the field.

The American team's strikers are power players. Alex Morgan is one of the captains and top scorers. She has the skills to race past defenders, or make the perfect pass. She also plays for the San Diego Wave of the NWSL. Megan Rapinoe was the 2019 world player of the year. Her **free kicks** often score or lead to goals for her team. Tobin Heath is a great dribbler. She takes on defenders before racing toward the goal. All three players helped the United States win two World Cups.

America's key midfielders are the defensive-minded Julie Ertz and the creative Rose Lavelle. Sam Mewis is a terrific two-way player who will be a star in the future.

On defense, Becky Sauerbrun has been the key player in the center since 2012. Young left-footer Tierna Davidson often teams with her to prevent attacks and goals.

Morgan, Lavelle, and Rapinoe pose with their trophies from the 2019 Women's World Cup.

Although they are not as successful as the women's team, the U.S. Men's National Team has some serious talent. The best player is Christian Pulisic, known for his lightning speed and ability to score. The Americans depend on him to beat the goalie in big games. He also stars for Chelsea in the Premier League.

Weston McKennie is a rising star at midfield. Before he was 23, he had played six pro seasons in Germany and Italy. You don't earn a place in those leagues unless you're really good!

McKennie has the ability to play several positions. He is quickly becoming one of the go-to guys for the U.S.

Pulisic helped Chelsea win the 2021 Champions League.

McKennie can do it all. He has played center back, midfield, and even scored at forward.

Tyler Adams also plays in Germany and is becoming a key part of the U.S. team.

In 2021, all three players were among a record 12 Americans who reached the Champions League.

Who do you think the next world soccer superstar will be?

McKennie was the first American to play for Juventus, one of the top teams in Italy.

GLOSSARY

agility (uh-JILL-ih-tee) ability to be fast, flexible, and move quickly in any direction

captain (KAP-tin) in sports, the player chosen to lead and represent his or her team

Champions League (CHAMP-ee-unz LEEG) an annual competition among the top pro soccer clubs in Europe

chip (CHIP) a short shot or pass that loops over a defender's head

crosses (KROSS-ez) passes that come from the corner of the soccer field to the area in front of the goal

defender (duh-FEN-der) a player who tries to stop the other team from scoring

dominate (DOM-ih-nayt) completely control

donate (DOH-nayt) give money or time to help someone

endurance (en-DUR-unss) ability to be physically active for a long period of time

formations (fore-MAY-shuns) the plans for where players are arranged on a sports field

free kicks (FREE KIX) plays given to a team after a foul is called

penalty box (PEN-ul-tee BOX) an area 18 yards in front of each goal in which the goalies are allowed to use their hands

penalty kick (PEN-ul-tee KIK) shot taken from 12 yards in front of the goal after a defensive foul is called in the penalty box

professional (pruh-FESH-un-ull) a person who is paid to play a sport

saves (SAYVZ) plays in which a goalie blocks a shot that would otherwise have gone into the goal

stepover dribbling (STEP-oh-ver DRIBB-ling) quick, back-and-forth movement by the feet over the ball as the players moves with it down the field

trapping (TRAP-ing) the skill of stopping the ball without using the hands

THINK ABOUT IT

Who was your favorite player in this book? Explain your answer.

What is your favorite soccer team? Why?

If you could play any position in soccer, which would you choose? Why?

FIND OUT MORE

IN THE LIBRARY

Doeden, Matt. *The World Cup: Soccer's Global Championship*. Minneapolis, MN: Millbrook Press, 2021.

Everything You Need to Know About Soccer. New York, NY: DK Publishing, 2022.

Weakland, Mark. *Soccer Records*. Mankato, MN: Black Rabbit Books, 2022

ON THE WEB

Visit our website for links about soccer superstars:
childsworld.com/links

Note to Parents, Teachers, and Librarians: We routinely verify our Web links to make sure they are safe and active sites. So encourage your readers to check them out!

INDEX

ABOUT THE AUTHOR

CHARLES SCHOENHERR was a middle-school and elementary-school language arts teacher in Colorado. He now works in marketing for a company that sells outdoor gear. He was a star soccer player in high school, and still follows the sport very closely, including his favorite team, Newcastle United, which plays in England.